LET'S VISIT CHINA

Let's visit

CHINA

DISCARD

LIAO HUNG-YING
AND
DEREK BRYAN

BURKE

First published October 1966
Reprinted January 1968
Second revised edition February 1973
Third revised edition November 1978
Fourth revised edition 1983

ACKNOWLEDGEMENTS

The Authors and Publishers are grateful to the following individuals and organisations for permission to reproduce copyright illustrations in this book:
    The Anglo-Chinese Education Institute; the late J. Allan Cash; Fotolink Picture Library; the late Stuart Gelder; Richard and Sally Greenhill; Keystone Press Agency Ltd.; Colin Penn; Paul Popper Lotd.
The cover illustration of the Drum Tower at Xian is reproduced by permission of the late J. Allan Cash.

CIP data
Hung-Ying, Liao
    Let's visit China. –4th ed.
    (1.) China – Social life and customs – Juvenile
    literature
    I. Title   II. Bryan, Derek
    951.05'8   DS779.23   *MD 88 10012*
    ISBN 0 222 00915 2

Burke Publishing Company Limited
Pegasus House, 116–120 Golden Lane, London EC1Y 0TL, England.
Burke Publishing (Canada) Limited
Toronto, Ontario, Canada.
Burke Publishing Company Inc.
540 Barnum Avenue, Bridgeport, Connecticut, 06608, U.S.A.
Filmset in 'Monophoto' Baskerville by Green Gates Studios, Hull, England.
Printed in Singapore by Tien Wah Press (Pte) Ltd.

Contents

Notes on Pronunciation

x sounds like **sh** in **she**
q sounds like **ch** in **cheer**
z sounds like **ds** in **reads**
c sounds like **ts** in **cats**
zh sounds like **dg** in **judge**
ai sounds like **igh** in **high**
e sounds like **er** in **her**
iang sounds like **young**

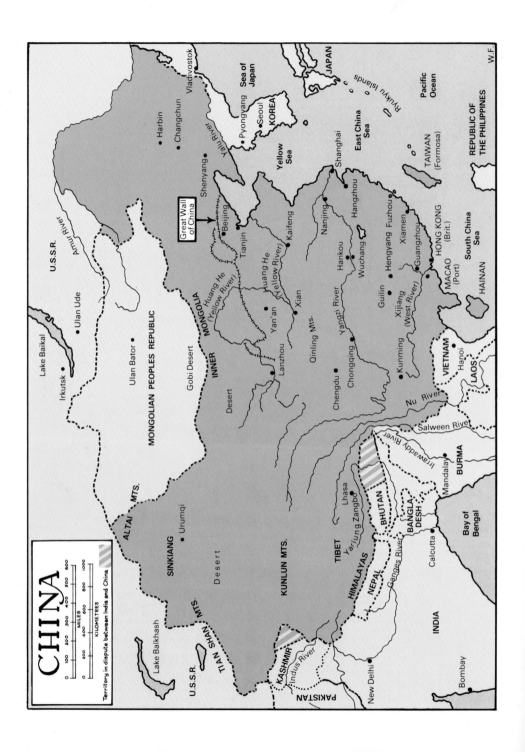

Let's Visit China

For hundreds of years, ever since Marco Polo brought back reports of the wonderful cities and great civilisation he had found in Cathay, Europeans have been fascinated by China. The art of making fine porcelain was first discovered there; when it first came to us in the West it was called *china-ware*, and then simply *china*. It was from China that silk came to Rome two thousand years ago, along the Silk Road through the heart of central Asia, taking years to reach its destination.

Tea came later, overland to Russia, and by sea to western Europe. Towards the end of the nineteenth century, in the last days of sailing-ships, the tea clippers did the journey from China to England in less than three months, which was then considered very fast. Today, you can get by air from many countries to China's capital Beijing (Peking) in less than twenty-four hours; thousands of people do this every week.

But we must content ourselves with an imaginary visit, trying to learn about the country and the people, to picture what it looks like from the inside, and to feel what it is like to be Chinese and live in China.

What is the land of China like? Covering almost four million square miles (over ten million square kilometres), it is the third largest country in the world, after the Soviet Union and Canada. The general lie of the land slopes down from west to east; the highest mountains are in the south-west and far west, forming part of the Himalayas, Pamirs, Tian Shan ("Mountains of Heaven") and Altai. These and other ranges are shared by China with India, Nepal, Pakistan, Afghanistan, Outer Mongolia and the Soviet Union. The highest peak in the world (which the Chinese call Qomolangma and we call Everest) lies between Nepal and China.

Most of west and north-west China is difficult country to live in, and the population is scattered. Tibet is largely a high plateau, with a bitterly cold climate for most of the year. To the north lies Xinjiang, much of which is desert. To the east of Xinjiang and Tibet, but still part of China's vast north-west, lie Qinghai, Gansu and the western part of Inner Mongolia. A great part of these regions is also Gobi, or desert, but all of them, like Tibet and Zinjiang, also have pastoral land, where sheep, horses and (in Tibet) yaks graze.

The three north-eastern provinces, known to us as Manchuria, besides very rich forest, include one of China's three great plains, the North-East Plain. The Daqing oilfield, China's mainstay of the industry, is located in the northernmost province, Heilongjiang. The Yellow River (Huang He), China's second longest river flows from its source in the mountains of Qinghai through a fertile *loess* (yellow earth) plateau, and finally through the North China plain into the sea. The Yellow River valley, in which the main crop is wheat, was the cradle of Chinese civilisation over five thousand years ago.

The 3,500-mile (5,600 kilometres) long Yangzi, China's

longest river, is the fourth longest in the world. Although, like the Yellow River, it makes many twists and turns, its basic course is from west to east. In its upper reaches it has to cut its way through high mountains, forming the famous Yangzi Gorges. Just below them, at Gezhouba, the river has been dammed to form a great complex of flood-gates, power-station and locks. This withstood a big flood and began to generate electricity in 1981. There are plans for an even bigger dam in the Gorges. Here a dam might one day be built to form the biggest hydro-electric power source in the world. It is in the Middle and Lower Yangzi Plain, and in the Pearl River valley in the south, that most of China's rice is grown.

The majority of Chinese people, like most of the peoples of south-east Asia, eat rice as their main cereal. The more nourishing wheat, traditionally preferred by northern Chinese, is gradually being grown and consumed in greater quantities. It is eaten mainly in the form of noodles (which Marco Polo

Drying fine noodles, near Chongqing

Picking tea near Hangzhou. Tea is one of eastern China's main crops

may have brought to Italy, thus introducing spaghetti!), steamed bread and flat griddle-cakes, although baked bread is becoming more popular in the cities.

Most of China south of the Yangzi is mountainous. The three great plains we have already mentioned form only about one-eighth of the total land surface. Because of this, and because the climate is generally more favourable, three-quarters of all the people live on less than a quarter of the land. They are concentrated mostly in the plains of north China, the Yangzi valley, the Zhujiang (Pearl River) valley in the south around Guangzhou (Canton), and the Chengdu plain, in the mid-west, which is surrounded by mountains.

These large populations are almost all *Han* people; i.e., the people whom we in the west call simply *Chinese*. The Chinese today number about 1,000 million people. The Chinese people also include about 70 million who belong to many national minorities. Some of these minority peoples, such as the Tibetans, Mongolians and Uygurs (Turkis), number millions, and are closely related to people who live across China's borders in neighbouring countries. Others of these minority communities are very small, some of them numbering only a few thousand.

China's total population of over 1,000 million is eighteen times as large as that of Britain. But its area is forty times as large as the total area of the United Kingdom. You can see from these figures that, as China develops her wide open spaces and rich natural resources, there will be plenty of room for her population, the rise in which is slowing down.

The Han Chinese people have sometimes been ruled in the past by non-Han people—such as the Mongolians and the Manchus—but Chinese civilisation and culture is chiefly that of the Hans. This book is about China as a whole, but in talking about the Chinese people we shall mainly be talking of the Hans who form the great majority.

What is China?

We have seen something of the land of China—its mountains, rivers and different peoples. But what about the land and people of the China we read about in books and newspapers, hear about on the radio and television, or see on films?

We sometimes see films with Chinese villains, wearing "pig-tails", smoking opium and carrying long knives. It is true that, up to 1911, Chinese men *did* wear their hair in long single plaits. They were made to do so by the Manchus, their foreign rulers, who invaded China from the north-east in 1644 and overthrew the Chinese imperial Ming dynasty. The pigtail was regarded as a badge of shame, and the Chinese cut off their pigtails when the Manchu empire was overthrown and the Republic of China established, in 1911.

In the same way, patriotic Chinese always regarded opium-smoking as something peculiarly shameful, because it could not be separated in their minds from foreign domination of China. Although opium had been introduced originally in the seventeenth century as a medicine to counteract malaria, dysentery, cholera and other diseases, people soon took to it as a drug.

By the early nineteenth century opium had become an essential part of British trade with China, to pay for the tea and silk so much in demand in Britain. The Manchu emperors tried to keep out foreign trade and foreign traders, but they were too weak to stop the growing imports of opium. These became so large that Chinese exports of tea and silk were not sufficient to pay for them and great quantities of silver had to be sent out of the country as well.

It became necessary to tax the ordinary peasant farmers more and more heavily in order to obtain this silver. As a

Throughout China there are many pagodas like this one in Shanxi. They were originally built to house Buddhist scriptures or other sacred objects

result, the imperial officials concerned with the opium trade became more and more corrupt as they pocketed their share of the spoil. In 1839 the emperor appointed a patriotic official to suppress the opium trade. He seized and burned 20,000 chests of opium at Canton (Guangzhou). This was the property of British, Indian and American merchants.

The British government under Lord Palmerston seized the opportunity of forcing China to open her cities to foreign trade, and in the following year landed troops. So began the war which the Chinese called the Opium War. Though many of the Chinese soldiers fought bravely, they were easily defeated by the British soldiers who were better trained and better equipped.

Under the Treaty of Nanking (Nanjing), signed in 1842 after the Chinese defeat, China had to pay the British expenses for the war, as well as the cost of the opium that had been burned. The total was 21 million silver dollars. In addition, Hong Kong became a British colony, and British people in China

13

were no longer bound to pay Chinese taxes, or to submit to Chinese law. British goods could be imported into China freely at a very low rate of Customs duty and five Chinese ports were opened to foreign trade. Other foreign powers joined in the "game" and, for over a hundred years, China was at their mercy. This situation continued until the country became fully independent again, in 1949.

During these hundred years, the Chinese people rose many times against their own rulers and against the aggressive foreigner. The familiar picture of Chinese equipped with long knives to use in attacking foreigners comes from one of these revolts, the Boxer Rebellion of 1900. This idea is as out of date as the idea of pigtailed and opium-smoking Chinese. No one smokes opium in China today (though some Chinese and other people smoke it in Hong Kong, Macao and other places ruled by non-Chinese governments).

From this it is easy to see that the picture we have had of the Chinese people was often not a true one. But nowadays it is much easier to know what people mean when they talk about China as a country, or a state, or a nation, and we no longer hear so much about "Communist China" or "Red China" on the one hand, and "Nationalist China" on the other.

Traditionally, the Chinese always referred to their country as *Zhongguo*, which means the "Central Kingdom". China was indeed the centre of the civilised world at a time when Europe was still in the Dark Ages. Its name comes from the first imperial dynasty of *Qin* (Chin) whose first emperor unified

14

Soil for new terraced fields being carried up the hillside. Modern China needs to cultivate as much land as possible to grow food for her vast population

China in 221 B.C. In 206 B.C. the Chin dynasty was followed by the Han dynasty (from which the Han Chinese people take their name) which ruled China for more than four hundred years, until A.D. 220.

In the centuries which followed, the country was often broken up under the rule of minor or major princes who fought with each other for power, rather like Christian Europe after the break-up of the Holy Roman Empire. But again and again China was unified, first under the great Tang and Song dynasties in the seventh and tenth centuries, then by Mongol invaders from the north (the Yuan or "Original" dynasty) in the thirteenth century and again under a Chinese dynasty (the Ming or "Bright") in the fourteenth century.

Finally, as we have already seen, the Ming rulers were replaced in 1644 by another foreign dynasty—that of the Manchus, who called their dynasty Qing (Ching), meaning "Pure". Although they had a period of greatness, they were quite unable to meet the challenge of the modern world, which came to them with the arrival of invaders, both from west and east. Throughout the nineteenth century the Chinese people, and above all the peasants, suffered increasing misery and degradation under their corrupt and inefficient rulers. If it had not been for the foreign powers who propped up the dynasty, it would have collapsed much earlier. When it did fall, in 1911, no one regretted its end.

The leader of the revolution which established the Republic

of China was Dr. Sun Yat-sen, a patriotic idealist who had been trained as a doctor in Hong Kong. He wanted to introduce Western methods of government, modern science, education and industry into China. But the people who had the power were the military commanders, or warlords, and they wanted to carve out little kingdoms for themselves, just as other military commanders had done in China for centuries past. Again and again Sun Yat-sen asked the governments of Britain, the United States and other Western powers for help, but they preferred to support warlord "strong men".

So, in 1923, Dr. Sun turned to Soviet Russia for help, and reorganised his Guomindang (Nationalist) party, accepting into it members of the Chinese Communist Party. With the aid of Russian military advisers, a military academy was founded near Canton with Chiang Kai-shek as President and the young Communist leader Zhou Enlai as Dean of Studies.

In 1926 the revolutionary armies marched north from Canton under the command of Chiang Kai-shek. They had wide popular support, and easily defeated the warlord armies.

But, in April 1927, in the hour of triumph, Chiang Kai-shek turned for help to his old friends the bankers of Shanghai and their foreign backers. With their support, he attacked and killed thousands of communists and workers.

The communist-led armies gained popular support and finally won supremacy. By 1949, Chiang had been forced to withdraw his remaining troops to the Chinese island of Taiwan (Formosa), and the People's Republic of China was

17

established on 1st October 1949, with Mao Zedong as Chairman and Zhou Enlai as Prime Minister.

The People's Republic, a developing Third World nation, is now recognised by almost every other country in the world as the only real China, but in Taiwan the old regime (often called "Nationalist China") still survives under American protection. For over twenty years Taiwan occupied China's seat in the United Nations but in 1971 the United States was defeated in the General Assembly by the overwhelming majority of the Third World countries, and the representatives of the People's Republic of China at last took their place. History had already given its clear verdict for Mao and against Chiang Kai-shek, who died four years later. In January 1976, Zhou Enlai died. In September, (a few weeks after the disastrous Tangshan earthquake which had killed almost a quarter of a million people) Mao Zedong died. An era had come to an end in China.

How China is Governed

China is divided administratively into twenty-two provinces, five autonomous regions and three cities directly under the central government. These are Beijing, the northern capital, Shanghai, the largest city, and Tianjin. Then there are almost

2,000 counties (including autonomous counties) and municipalities. The counties are in turn subdivided into rural townships.

The autonomous regions are vast areas, three of which (Xinjiang, Inner Mongolia and Tibet) are larger than the largest provinces. The autonomous regions (and a number of autonomous counties under some provinces) have been set up wherever people of national minorities live in compact communities.

The provinces and regions of China may be grouped together in various different ways. In this book we have divided them as follows:

1. Beijing (the capital), Hebei province (in which Beijing is situated) and Shanxi province, to the west of Hebei.

A boy of the Yi national minority

2. The three north-eastern provinces (Heilongjiang, Jilin and Liaoning, which used to be known as Manchuria) and the neighbouring autonomous region of Inner Mongolia.

3. The four eastern coastal provinces of Shandong, Jiangsu (in which Shanghai is situated), Zhejiang and Fujian; the neighbouring province of Anhui; and the island province of Taiwan (Formosa).

4. "Central China"—the four provinces of Jianxsi, Hunan, Hubei and Henan.

5. The north-west (Shaanxi, Gansu and Qinghai provinces) and the Ningxia and Xinjiang autonomous regions.

6. The south-west (Sichuan, Guizhou and Yunnan provinces) and the Tibet autonomous region.

7. Guangdong province and the Gwangxi autonomous region.

The system of political representation in China is indirect. This means that the voters at the lowest level—adult members of a township, or residents of a municipal district or members of the armed forces—elect their local congress. Members of these local congresses elect those of counties and municipalities, the counties and municipalities those of the provinces, and the provinces (together with the autonomous regions and the cities of Beijing, Tiantjin and Shanghai) elect the members of the National People's Congress.

Day-to-day business at each level is administered by councils elected by the congresses. The central executive body is the State Council or Central People's Government, which co-ordinates the various ministries. The Chairman of the People's Republic, elected by the National People's Congress, is the Head of State.

Beijing, the Capital

Beijing (Peking) was the capital of China under many dynasties, especially the Yuan (Mongols), the Ming, and the Qing (Manchus). We have often heard of the "Forbidden City", which was the winter palace of the Manchu emperors. Ordinary people were forbidden even to go near its gates, hence the name Forbidden City. Now it is open to the public and contains many museums. The buildings are not at all like the museums we know. They are really a series of buildings, separated by courtyards—some very large—and alley-ways. The Forbidden City, like Beijing as a whole, is symmetrical,

This marble staircase leads up to the "Hall of Supreme Harmony" in the former Forbidden City

the east matching the west. The main gate is at the south and is called Tian An Men ("The Gate of Heavenly Peace"). On 1st October 1949, Chairman Mao Zedong stood on this gate to announce the establishment of the Chinese People's Republic; since then, 1st October has been China's National Day.

The Art Museum in the Forbidden City contains priceless articles of jade and magnificent prehistoric painted pottery, more than four thousand years old; it also has on display the famous Tang pottery horses and countless other treasures. The variety and beauty of the porcelain is almost breathtaking. The paintings are not so easy for us to appreciate. They are water-colours on silk or paper in the form of scrolls which are rolled up to keep out dust and sunlight. The older paintings—some over a thousand years old—are difficult to make out, as the colour of the silk has darkened. Some are fascinating; one of them is very long, with scenes of villages, houses and people doing their daily work on the banks of a river, with boats sailing by.

Outside the northern gate of the Forbidden City is a hill facing south, sometimes called by the strange name of Coal Hill (because there was a legend that coal was buried beneath it). Here, in 1644, the last Ming emperor hanged himself, shortly before the Manchu armies captured Peking. Today the Coal Hill is a favourite playground for children. If we go to the top, stand in the middle and look southwards, the view is a long straight line of buildings and courtyards, with lanes and rows of buildings on both sides. The whole palace is a work of art based on a rectangular design, demonstrating the Chinese sense of space and proportion.

Coming out of the Tian An Men (the main gate), we face the very wide Chang An Street and the huge square to the south of it. On the Chinese National Day and on May Day the people celebrate with gatherings and parties in the nearby parks. There is a lot of singing and dancing, gymnastics, Chinese "shadow boxing" and fencing, sports events, theatre and cinema shows.

On the east side of the square stands the Historical Museum; on the west, the Great Hall of the People. This is huge. Its main Conference Hall has seats for 10,000, and the main

A summer view
of old Beijing

Banqueting Hall can accommodate 5,000 people. There are many other halls for meetings of different sizes, and numerous rooms for committees, for relaxation, and for the actors to make up in when theatrical performances are presented.

In the south centre of the square is the Mao Zedong Memorial Hall, an imposing building completed in 1977 to which every part of China contributed something distinctive. It houses the embalmed body and a marble statue of him.

On the north-east side of the square, next door to the Forbidden City, is the Workers' Palace, where the people go on Sundays with their families, to read, paint, dance, play chess, etc. There are tutors to help them if needed.

There are many very old trees in the garden of the Workers' Palace (formerly the Imperial Ancestors' Temple). In Beijing there are many other parks and folk-art centres and, of course, there is the world-famous Temple of Heaven where the emperor used to offer sacrifices every spring asking Heaven to bestow a good harvest on the whole empire.

The covered Dong An Market is nearly always crowded and is a fascinating place where much bargaining used to go on. Now all prices are fixed. East of the City is a fine new Workers' Stadium, seating 100,000 people.

West of the city there is the zoo, where the first giant panda bred in captivity was born. In the western and north-western suburbs of Beijing there are dozens of colleges and institutes of learning. Except for Beijing University and Tsinghua University, they were all established after 1949.

Near to the universities is the Summer Palace. Built for the

Manchu Dowager Empress, it is now a public park. Here people come in their thousands to swim, walk and picnic.

The farms around Beijing mostly grow fruit and vegetables for the capital. During the very cold winter, vegetables are grown in pits under glass, so that there is still a plentiful supply of fresh food. Poultry, pigs and dairy cows are also raised.

Beijing, being the capital, has restaurants which serve regional dishes from all over the country. Northern Chinese cooking is generally plainer than that of the south, but the strong flavours of onion and garlic are popular. Mutton and beef are eaten, as well as pork which is the most popular meat in the country as a whole. The people of Sichuan, Guizhou, Hunan and Yunnan eat dishes which are highly seasoned with red pepper. In the south-east, the popular taste is for more delicate flavours.

Of all Chinese foods perhaps the most typical is bean-curd—a nutritious product which is prepared in many different ways. All over the country, of course, and even outside China—in Japan, Korea, Vietnam and much of south-east Asia—people eat with chopsticks, which are easier to use than knives and forks!

About twenty miles (32 kilometres) north-west of Beijing runs the Great Wall of China. It was built about 2,200 years ago to mark the boundary between the Mongolian grasslands and the settled farmlands of the Han people in North China. The Wall stretches for a considerable distance from Shanhai-

A section of the Great Wall of China

guan (on the coast, east of Beijing) to the far west of Gansu province in the north-west. It runs seemingly endlessly over mountains and valleys and has fortress towers at regular intervals; parts of it are now broken or tumbled down. The section nearest Beijing was repaired soon after 1949. It is a very popular

26

place for outings. The Wall is so thick that the top is like a broad hilly road, sometimes so steep that it is built in steps. The view from the top is magnificent, as the eye follows the Wall over peaks and slopes; the Wall stretches as far as one can see.

The province in which Beijing is situated is called Hebei ("North of the River"—meaning the Yellow River). Its fertile plain, which stretches eastwards to the sea, is thickly populated. The great river port and industrial city of Tianjin trades with many parts of the world, and foreign ships call there regularly. To the south-east, Hebei borders on the province of Shandong ("East of the Mountains"); to the south is Henan ("South of the River").

In the north and west of Hebei are high mountains, which rise to 10,000 feet (over 3,000 metres) on the borders of Shanxi ("West of the Mountains") province. Shanxi's western and southern borders are formed by the Yellow River.

Travelling in China

What is travelling in China today like? Visitors from Europe going by the shortest route first see the Great Wall from the air as they fly into Beijing from Moscow by way of Mongolia. Or they may travel the same route by train.

Either way is exciting, especially the first sight of the Great Wall. Or again they may travel the longer way by train, through the wide open spaces of north-east China, and come into Peking from the east.

Another way, which many visitors find convenient, is to fly in from Europe or Japan to Shanghai or Beijing. But more people go into China by way of Hong Kong than by any other route.

Hong Kong is really a little part of China still under foreign rule. Within its 400 square miles (over 1,000 square kilometres), 4,500,000 people live crowded together, including some who are very rich and many who are very poor. It has a magnificent natural harbour; for over a hundred years much of the trade between China and Europe went through Hong Kong. Since the end of the Second World War, Chinese from overseas and others have invested large sums of money in Hong Kong, which is now an important industrial centre, exporting its products all over the world.

Ninety-nine people out of a hundred in Hong Kong, including the workers in the factories and most of the business-men, are Chinese. For all its great skyscrapers, American films and western cars, Hong Kong still looks what it is, a Chinese city. Because of this, people who have visited or lived there sometimes say they have been to China.

A short train journey of an hour or so takes the traveller from Hong Kong to the Chinese border. A walk across the bridge over the narrow river and you are in the Shenzhen station, in the People's Republic of China. From here a Chinese train takes you to Canton in a few hours.

From Guangzhou there is a choice of several routes north. The quickest is by air, via Wuhan or Shanghai, but the train is more interesting. The direct line to Beijing is over 1,400 miles (2,250 kilometres) long. It goes due north, crossing the Yangzi River from Wuchang to Hankou by the famous Wuhan Bridge. A longer route, branching off two-thirds of the way to Wuhan, leads by way of Hangzhou to Shanghai, crosses the Yangzi at Nanjing, and eventually arrives in Beijing through Tianjin.

These train journeys are long—the shortest time for the 1,450 miles (2,320 kilometres) from Guangzhou to Beijing is $33\frac{1}{2}$ hours, and you eat and sleep on the train—but they are full of interest. North of Guangzhou the line winds through minor gorges of reddish rock to cross over the watershed into Hunan province. In summer the whole journey is hot, but in winter it gets much cooler as you go northwards. In the Yangzi valley there is often snow, and farther north winters are bitterly cold, though there is bright sunshine most of the time.

From South China up to the Yangzi, and for some distance farther north, rice is the main crop; from the train you may see it being sown, transplanted or harvested, at different seasons. In the south, the growing season lasts all year round, and two or three crops a year are grown. North of the Yangzi the line goes through China's cotton- and wheat-growing areas.

The Beijing-Guangzhou express, making its way through some of China's most beautiful countryside

The whole journey reminds one of a scroll painting, unfolding a slowly changing panorama of the Chinese landscape. In this wide panorama, the people are sometimes hardly to be seen; yet the line passes through some of the most populous parts of China. From time to time, though, little groups of men and women can be seen, walking along the raised paths between the rice fields, weeding, cultivating, applying fertiliser or harvesting. Seeing these little groups, it is difficult to realise that, with their families, the peasant farmers number more than 850 million throughout China.

When you get out of the train and start to walk around Guangzhou, Shanghai or Beijing, the streets are very crowded, like big cities everywhere. As in Hong Kong, there is an air of bustle, and the people are Chinese, but there the resemblance ends. There are not many cars, but a lot of buses and trolley-buses (nearly always crowded) and thousands upon thousands of bicycles. The old two-wheeled rickshaws pulled by men have gone, but there are still three-wheeled bicycle rickshaws (pedicabs) carrying mainly goods.

All kinds of goods are transported through the streets in lorries, in carts drawn by horses, donkeys, mules—and by people. Compared with the West, China is still poor and technically backward; much work still has to be done without the aid of machines, especially in the countryside. But everyone has food, clothing and shelter, and in cities all children go to school. In rural areas the problem is more difficult, because some peasants tend to keep their children, especially daughters, at home to help with house or farm work. The Government try to change their attitudes, but it is a rather slow process.

The North-east and Inner Mongolia

North-east China was the homeland of the Manchu people who ruled over China from 1644 to 1911. Many of them, including the emperors, studied the Han language and literature; some became great scholars.

The Manchurian climate is very cold in winter. The Amur or Heilungjiang (Black Dragon River) and Songhuajing (Sungari), bordering on the Soviet Union, are frozen for many months of the year.

In the north and north-west are the Xing'an Mountains with rich forests and many wild animals. Some parts are now protected reserves, so that rare animals can be kept and studied. A large timber industry and forestry research institute have been established here for balanced felling and re-planting.

South of these mountains the soil is rather like that of the prairies of North America and is very rich. The main crops are sorghum (giant millet), wheat and soya beans. In recent years sugar beet has been more widely grown, as has rice, which is generally regarded as needing a hot and wet climate.

There are rich coal and iron deposits in this part of China. In 1931, the Japanese imperial troops seized the whole of

A bountiful harvest of grain. The farmers are wearing thick padded clothes to protect them from the cold north-eastern climate

Pu Yi, the last Emperor of China, died an ordinary citizen in 1967

north-east China. They built iron and steel works and used the products for their own purposes. They also shipped a lot of grain and coal to Japan. But this industry started by the Japanese was very small compared with what has been developed since 1949.

During their occupation the Japanese set up a puppet state which they called *Manchukuo* ("Kingdom of the Manchus") with the last emperor of the Qing Dynasty, Aisin-Gioro Pu Yi, as a figurehead. When Japan surrendered in 1945, the emperor was, of course, taken prisoner by the Soviet troops. He was then turned over to the Chinese for a further term.

Some years later he was released from prison and he then worked in a botanical garden in Beijing, and in a historical research institute. Later, he wrote his autobiography,

33

translated into English under the title *From Emperor to Citizen*. In this book he claimed that he had never enjoyed life when he was an emperor—having nominal power but no freedom—as much as when he became a free citizen.

The Inner Mongolian autonomous region lies between the People's Republic of Mongolia in the north and the Great Wall in the south. It has the Gobi Desert in the north-west and the Ordos Desert in the south-west. Huhehot is the capital. Many of the people here are nomadic and are wonderful horsemen.

The long history of relations between the Mongolian and the Han peoples is not a happy one. In ancient days the various northern nomadic tribes constantly raided the Han villages or invaded wide stretches of territory—rather like the Scots and the English on the border—while the Han farmers encroached on the Mongolian land. Thick and high walls were built to keep the tribes out and keep the Hans in; it was these which were eventually joined up as the Great Wall of China.

Kublai Khan, grandson of the Mongol conqueror Genghis Khan, conquered China and became the first emperor of the Yuan dynasty (1274–1368). This did not improve the relationship of the two peoples. The ruling Mongolian officials oppressed the Han people and, as a result, aroused their hatred. Culturally, the Mongolians were a much younger people; they were also less experienced in trade and it was easy for the Han merchants to cheat them.

34

Watering horses (Inner Mongolia)

In more modern times, in the twentieth century, the Mongolians suffered badly under the warlords and later under Chiang Kai-shek's régime. Many of them joined the Chinese Red Army, led by the Communists. In this army they fought against the Japanese occupation forces and, later, against Chiang Kai-shek.

Under the People's Government, Inner Mongolia was granted the status of an autonomous (self-governing) region. The people have greatly developed their economic and cultural life. With the aid of science, the grasslands are being improved and silage (the preservation of green fodder) has been introduced. To ensure water supplies, deep wells have been dug and the number of electric water-pumps in operation is continually increasing. The herdsmen have built more permanent houses, schools and hospitals. They now no longer have to move their cattle and sheep all the time in order to find grazing for them. With better fodder and the introduction of veterinary service, the number of animals increases from year to year.

In addition, Baotou, near the centre of Inner Mongolia, has one of the largest iron and steel plants in China. Many other kinds of industry are growing in this area, especially canning, leather and wool.

There are still many herdsmen in remote parts of the region but, even here, some social amenities are available. There are school teachers who often travel long distances on horseback to bring schooling to the children. Music and drama groups, medical teams and trade teams constantly travel in the region, visiting the yurts (tents made of felt stretched over a framework) which form the traditional homes of the Mongolians.

It is not an uncommon sight in this region to see four horses pulling a cart, or a line of camels ridden by a group of young men and women, struggling over mountains, rivers, deserts or sand-dunes. They are the Ulan Muchir teams (Red Cultural troupes) who travel in all weathers to perform their plays, operas and dances for the herdsmen and farmers.

Eastern China

The four provinces of Shandong, Jiangsu, Zhejiang and Fujian have a long coastline extending from about 38° North to the Tropic of Cancer in the south. Their climate ranges from the temperate climate of Shandong to the semi-tropical climate of Fujian. Shandong and Jiangsu include both extensive plains and some mountains; Zhejiang and Fujian are largely mountainous. The products of the four provinces range from wheat, apples, pears, grapes and peanuts in the north, to rice, silk, tea, timber, bamboo and semi-tropical fruits in the south. The region is densely populated, especially in the delta of the Yangzi River, which flows through Jiangsu into the sea. China's other world-famous river, the Yellow River (which used to be known as China's Sorrow, because of the way it flooded very large areas of land and drowned millions of people), enters the sea in Shandong.

The famous Grand Canal, the building of which began over two thousand years ago, also passes through Shandong. It is about 1,080 miles (1,728 kilometres) long and links Beijing with Hangzhou, crossing the Yellow River and the Yangzi. It was a very important waterway, along which grain, silk, porcelain and other products were conveyed from the provinces to the capital. In the nineteenth century it was neglected and fell into disuse, but since 1949 it has been dredged, deepened and widened to take steamers in some sections.

The province of Shandong, which sticks out into the sea, is

China has been famous for centuries for her silk. These mulberry leaves are used to feed silkworms

one of the most populous in China, from which in the past many people emigrated to the north-east. In it is the birthplace of the great scholar of 2,500 years ago—Confucius. This name comes from the Chinese Kong Fuzi ("Kong the Teacher"). The most important part of his teaching was that concerned with the proper relationships between people; his ideas have influenced the Han people for over two thousand years. In every city in China, large or small, there was a Temple of Confucius where, in imperial times, a service was held once a year in his memory. The influence of Confucius's teachings also extended to China's neighbours, Japan, Korea and Vietnam, and continues to this day, as it does in China.

Jiangsu, Zhejiang and the inland province of Anhui

have much in common in climate and landscape. Though, like most of China, they are hot in the summer, for a large part of the year they have a climate rather like that of England, with some snow in winter and widespread rain throughout the year. The historic culture of the area has produced many great poets, painters and writers. And, for centuries, their silks were the best in the world.

The largest city in China, and fourth largest in the world, is Shanghai in Jiangsu province. Here there was formerly an International Settlement, whose tall buildings still make Shanghai look foreign. The International Settlement, like foreign concessions in other major Chinese cities, developed from 1840 onwards, when Britain, France, the United States of America and other Western countries (later also Japan) forced their way into China in spite of much opposition.

In those days, Shanghai was famous for thieves and gangsters, gamblers and kidnappers and was known as a Paradise for Adventurers. Every year tens of thousands died in the streets from hunger, cold and disease.

Now Shanghai is a very different place. Some of the gangsters fled abroad. Others, the smaller fry, have learned that they can earn an honest living by doing some hard work. Some of these people found it very hard to change their ways, but others took to the new life easily; in the old days, even they lived in constant fear and danger, because of the fierce competition within their own "profession".

Shanghai is still the largest industrial city in China. Many of the former small workshops have joined together to form bigger factories. Some have achieved remarkable feats in making delicate and complicated new tools, machines and scientific instruments, from the smallest surgical needle to giant presses. Many new factories have been built.

This rapid industrial development in Shanghai has gone hand in hand with advances in science, technology and education. From here every year large numbers of scientists and technicians go out to all parts of China to help in the work of development; similarly, many are sent to Shanghai for training.

Many parks, sports grounds and swimming-pools have been added to Shanghai in recent years, and Shanghai zoo is one of the finest in the world.

China has many rich fisheries along her coastline. This haul was brought in by a Shandong commune's fishing team

The many waterways in Suzhou are used for transporting both goods and people

Still in Jiangsu, and fifty miles (80 kilometres) west of Shanghai, is Suzhou, a much older city whose gardens have been famous for centuries. They include artificial rock hills, lakes, streams, bridges, pavilions and winding paths, as well as trees, shrubs and flowers. They were formerly part of the estates of wealthy scholars; house and garden together were surrounded by high walls, shutting them off from the outside world of the poor. Altogether there are over 150 of them, some of outstanding natural and architectural beauty.

Hangzhou, the capital of Zhejiang province, is a great tourist centre. Writing of it in the thirteenth century, Marco Polo described it as "without doubt the finest and most splendid city in the world". The West Lake has many picturesque bridges and pavilions with poems inscribed on the walls or on scrolls hung from the walls—the poems were written by visiting poets through the ages. A famous verse runs:

41

Fishermen on the West Lake at Hangzhou

Shang you Tiantang (In heaven above, Paradise,
Xia you Su, Hang. On earth, Suzhou, Hangzhou.)

The Chinese language is written in the form of "characters". Here is one of them 木 (pronounced *mu*) meaning "timber". Most of the characters are much more complicated than this, which makes the script very difficult to learn.

The northern dialect of the Han language spoken by most Chinese people used to be called "Mandarin", and is now called *putonghua* (common speech). It is generally spoken by people all over the country, although previously about one-third of the population spoke a variety of different local dialects. The Chinese also use the *pinyin* system (our alphabet but leaving out the letter "v") to spell their language phonetically, but they have not abandoned their expressive and beautiful system of writing in characters.

On the mountains grows the famous Dragon-Well tea. It is mixed with jasmine flowers and is said to taste best when made with water from the Dragon-Well spring.

North-west of Hangzhou is Nanjing ("the southern capital") the seat of the Jiangsu provincial government. Nanjing was often the national capital in the past, but never for very long. With the Yangzi River on one side and the Purple Mountain on another, it is situated in a strategic position. Outside the great city wall are the fine tombs of the first Ming emperor (1368–1398), and of Dr. Sun Yat-sen, the leader of the 1911 revolution, who died in 1925. The third and longest bridge over the Yangzi was completed in 1968 at Nanjing.

The Nanjing Bridge over the Yangzi River. At one time more than 50,000 people were working on its construction

Fuzhou, the capital of Fujian, is the home of the finest lacquer in the world. Built up from layer on layer of varnish on a base of fine gauze, it takes a very long time to make. Fujian province is one of the most beautiful in China, with its mountains and its rapid and dangerous rivers, which are being improved for navigation. Because of the mountains and the almost total lack of roads, there were no wheeled vehicles at all in some parts of this province for many centuries. Different districts have been so isolated that people of one locality could not understand the speech of those from another district. Many people emigrated abroad from Fujian.

In December 1956, a 440-mile (708 kilometres) railway was finished, the first in the history of the province.

Taiwan (Formosa is a name from the Portuguese meaning the "Beautiful Island") is about a hundred miles (160 kilometres) from the mainland. For centuries it was a part of Fujian province. About ninety per cent of the population of Taiwan are descendants of the Fujian people who went over to

An aqueduct irrigating a fertile plain in southern Fujian

the island during the centuries. The Japanese attacked China by land and sea in 1894 and then imposed a peace treaty, under which Taiwan became a Japanese colony. It was only returned to China at the end of the Second World War after the Japanese surrender. Even during the fifty years of Japanese occupation the relationship between the people in Fujian and in Taiwan remained close; there was much coming and going between "cousins", however distant. Since the beginning of the 1980s, contacts with the mainland have greatly increased.

North and South of the Middle Yangzi

To the west of Fujian lies the province of Jiangxi. Here the climate is continental—cold in winter and hot in summer. The soil is mostly red and not very fertile, but it is being gradually improved. Jiangxi is best known as the home of fine porcelain, made at Jingdezhen, east of the big Poyang Lake. Under the Manchu dynasty, the finest porcelain of all was sent to Beijing as tribute (i.e., as taxation paid in the form of goods). Other provinces had to send grain, copper for the coinage, fruits, and tribute silk—the fine brocades woven in east China.

To the east of Jiangxi, on the border with Fujian, are the mountains called Wuyi, the home of what was once a well-known tea. The Gan River flows from south to north through Jiangxi, into the Poyang Lake, and from there into the Yangzi. Farther west is Hunan province ("South of the—

Since rice is the staple food of China, fields like this one are a familiar sight in all fertile areas

Dongting—Lake"). Similarly, the Xiang River flows northwards through Hunan into the Dongting Lake, and thence into the Yangzi. The area around the Dongting Lake is a very fertile rice-growing district, sometimes known as the rice-bowl of China.

Hunan has a reputation for producing good soldiers, so it is not surprising to find that Mao Zedong, who worked out the strategy and tactics that won victory for the Chinese Red Armies, was born and bred there. He came from a peasant family and, as a young man in the 1920s, he made an intensive study of the peasants' problems, living and working among them. This study was the beginning of events which led to the greatest peasant revolution in world history.

North of Hunan, and astride the Yangzi, is the province of Hubei ("North of the—Dongting—Lake"). Its capital, the triple city of Wuhan (Wuchang, Hankou and Hanyang) is at the cross-roads, where the Yangzi is bridged by the Beijing–Guangzhou rail line. Wuhan is a large educational, industrial and communications centre, in which the most impressive construction is the Yangzi Bridge, of which the Chinese people are justly proud. They had always dreamed of a bridge over the wide river which steam ferries took twenty minutes to cross. Former governments invited German and American engineers to undertake surveys for this purpose, but the difficulties were so great that nothing was done.

Between 1955 and 1957, Chinese engineers, technicians and workers built the bridge, with the help of Soviet engineers, in twenty-six months. It is over a mile (1,600 metres) long, and so high that steamers can pass under it even at the highest water level ever recorded. It has two decks, the upper for motor traffic and the lower for trains.

This bridge is recognised as one of the great engineering achievements of the modern world.

To the north is the province of Henan ("South of the—Yellow—River") which belongs in climate to northern China. Historically it is the centre of Chinese civilisation. The city of Anyang was the capital of the Shang dynasty as early as the sixteenth century B.C. Articles dug out from the buried city, particularly bones and bronzes, have been studied, and the writings on them help us to find out about the life and customs of that ancient time, as well as to study the origins of the Chinese language itself. Many very fine bronze objects from

China's main east–west artery. the Yangzi River, is crossed at Yan'an by this great bridge linking north and south China by rail and road

Anyang and other places are on show in museums in Europe and in North America.

Although the soil in Henan can be very fertile, it needs water for its crops of wheat and cotton. In some years when there was too little rain, the crops failed because of drought; whatever water there was soaked away through the porous loess soil. In other years the Yellow River overflowed and brought disaster to thousands of people.

Because of the silt brought down from the upper reaches, the height of the river-bed rose each year. And each year the dikes had to be built higher to protect the villages and farmland. Even so, a really heavy flood would break the dikes. Thus, the people were left destitute, if they were not drowned, and they had to abandon their villages and roam about begging. For centuries, the people of Henan had to migrate south in order to keep themselves alive.

48

Now all this is a thing of the past. A great plan for harnessing the Yellow River is gradually being carried out, step by step, along its whole course. Dams, reservoirs, irrigation and drainage canals, power-stations and pumps are being built in their thousands, large and small. The river is being tamed and is being used for navigation, as well as for generating electric power. In its upper reaches, the hills are planted with trees, so that the precious soil is held firm instead of being washed away and helping to flood lower areas.

In the last forty years much Chinese history has been made in Jiangxi and Hunan. On 1st August 1927, army units stationed at Nanchang, the capital of Jiangxi province, rose against Chiang Kai-shek and formed an independent worker-peasant army. (This was the beginning of the Chinese Red Army which, for many years now, has been called the People's Liberation Army.) Soon afterwards, a group of guerrilla fighters was formed under the leadership of Mao Zedong at Jinggangshan—a mountainous region on the borders of Henan and Jiangxi provinces. In the following years many other groups also established themselves in border regions between different provinces, where Chiang Kai-shek's armies could not easily reach them. These border regions depended on the support of the local peasants.

By 1934 the pressure of Chiang Kai-shek's forces had become too great, and the Red Army decided to move to north-west China, where they would be in a good position to resist Japanese attacks. So they split up into different groups and started on the famous "Long March". By many twists and turns they covered some 8,000 miles (about 13,000 kilometres) before they arrived, a year later, in Shaanxi province. Many thousands died on the way, but many others joined them as they went along, and the March sowed the seeds of revolution all along its route.

The North-west

China's vast north-west includes the provinces of Shaanxi, Gansu and Qhinghai. It also includes two autonomous regions—Ningxia and Xinjiang—most of whose people are not Han Chinese. They belong to Moslem national minorities. For thousands of years the camel caravans of merchants trading in Chinese silk, which eventually reached Rome, passed through this area. They travelled along the "Silk Road", through what is called the Gansu Corridor (south of the Great Wall where it nears its end in the desert).

Centuries ago this was a fertile zone, well watered and with plenty of trees. But it gradually became drier and drier, and eventually desert, so that, finally, the road became a link between a few oases in a vast area of desert. The water is still there, but it is underground, and today the people have taken effective steps to put it to good use before it evaporates or runs away in the sands of the desert.

Lanzhou, the capital of Gansu province, is a geographical centre of China, and an important railway junction. From

50

here a short line leads west to Xining, capital of Qhinghai province, and another, much longer, goes north-west along the Gansu Corridor to Urumqi, capital of Xinjiang. Eventually, this line should link up with railways of the Soviet Union.

North-eastwards, along the western bank of the Yellow River, another line leads through Ningxia to link up with a railway from Beijing at Baotou, the big steel centre in Inner Mongolia. And south-east from Lanzhou runs the line to Xian, capital of Shaanxi province.

Except for a short stretch west of Xian, all these railways have been built since 1949. Hundreds of bridges had to be constructed, the lines protected from drifting desert sands or landslips, and many other engineering difficulties overcome. They are one of the outstanding achievements of modern China, and new railway lines continue to be built.

The city of Xian ("Western Peace") is today an industrial, educational and administrative centre, the biggest in the north-west. It was the capital of China under the Han dynasty for two centuries (221 B.C. to A.D. 9) and again for almost three centuries (A.D. 618 to 906) under the Tang dynasty, when it was the largest and richest city in the world. The beautiful little pottery figures (often seen in museums) which have been found in tombs of the Tang period often represent, besides Chinese people, Indian jugglers, Syrian singers and actors, Persian or Arab merchants; these were just a few of the many foreigners welcomed to the Tang capital.

For many centuries there was much coming and going

between China and other countries in Asia. Chinese influence had extended (by way of Korea) to Japan, to Vietnam and, along the "Silk Road", into central Asia (and thence to Rome) as early as the second century B.C., while the Buddhist religion was first brought to China from India in A.D. 67.

In the seventh century Chinese rule was established in Xinjiang (the "New Dominion"), known in the West as Chinese Turkestan. This vast area was then a stronghold of Buddhism, but in A.D. 75 a Chinese army was defeated by Moslem forces at the battle of the Talas River and the whole of central Asia fell to Islam.

Buddhism and Islam were not the only foreign religions in China in the great days of the Tang capital of Xian. Sun-worshipping Zoroastrians had come from Persia early in the sixth century; and, in about A.D. 600, Syrian monks brought Nestorian Christianity to China; a famous monument known as the Nestorian Stone is still to be seen in Xian today. Except for Buddhism and Islam, which did strike roots, all these religions flourished in China for a time and then died out.

In Xian, as elsewhere in China, the close link between modern China and its past is very clear. This link with the historical past is partly due to the strength, uniformity and continuity of Chinese culture and the Chinese sense of history. Besides being a fine modern city, Xian today is rich in historical relics and museums; the site of the large Tang palace is now being uncovered by archaeologists and, a short distance away, the capital of the Qin dynasty (221–207 B.C.)

is also being excavated. (It was the first Qin emperor who unified the feudal kingdoms into one country, and standardised the written language and system of government.)

In 1974, the most spectacular find of all was made by peasants digging a well near Xian. This was the vault containing six thousand life-size civil and military figures, on foot and on horseback, all modelled in clay—a "buried army" to defend the buried emperor. An endless stream of tourists visits this newly discovered wonder of the world.

In 1935, a little town in the mountains north of Xian began to attract people from all over China. This was Yan'an, where the Red Army ended their famous Long March from south-east China. In the poor mountainous areas around Yan'an, a new kind of social system was developed under the slogan "Serve the People". The army, led by Mao Zedong, Zhu De, Zhou Enlai and others, helped the peasants to improve their crops, developed handicraft production, taught people to read and write, and encouraged artists and actors to use their art in a way that all could appreciate.

The geography of China's north-west is very striking. Shensi, Ningsia and Kansu have a common bond in the loess soil, borne by the wind and deposited on the 3,000-foot-high (about 900 metres) plateau (which includes Shanxi province). There is very little rainfall in the area, which has long and sunny, but very cold winters. During the short summers, torrential rains

A street scene in Yan'an

wash away the precious topsoil, forming ever-widening and deepening barren gullies. For centuries the area was desperately poor. In the winter of 1943–44 the authors saw many children in Gansu almost naked, or in rags, at a time when the Yellow River was frozen so hard that cars and lorries could drive on it.

In some parts of the loess plateau people built themselves comfortable houses in caves, which were cool in summer and warm in winter. Mao Zedong and other communist leaders lived in such caves in Yan'an.

But farther north and west, the land becomes desert. Sand borne by the terrible biting north-west wind sometimes buried fertile fields, houses and even whole villages.

But today all this is changing. A continual fight is being waged against the encroaching desert; bit by bit, it is being won back to cultivation. Broad belts of trees have been planted over considerable distances, to shelter the fields and reduce the force of the winds. More are being planted every year. Parts of the Baotou-Lanzhou railway line are guarded from the sandstorms by an ingenious and complicated system of belts of grasses, bushes and trees.

In the past, the Moslem farmers, herdsmen and traders of the north-west suffered even more than the ordinary Han people from oppression by the government, local landlords and feudal rulers. There were many rebellions, suppressed with great bloodshed. Today, all the autonomous regions are

Hand-weeding in the north-west (near Yan'an)

Picking and drying cotton. Cotton is widely grown in north and north-west China. It is still the most important raw material for clothing (in winter, padded cotton suits are worn)

given specially favourable treatment by the central government to help their people raise themselves out of poverty and make their rightful contribution to the advance of the nation as a whole.

The natural products of the north-west are varied indeed. The crops include wheat, millet, highland barley (like that grown in Tibet), oil-seeds and rice; persimmons, apricots, fine melons and grapes; cotton, flax and silk. There is also wool from sheep and camels. And there are many large oilfields in the region (in Gansu, Qinghai and Xinjiang). The city of

Lanzhou which was a decayed and sleepy provincial town up until 1949, is now a centre of education, scientific research, industry and communications for the whole region.

Going west from Lanzhou it is only a short journey to Xining, the capital of Qinghai province, which is part of the Tibetan Plateau. Both the Yangzi River and the Yellow River have their sources in Qinghai which is a very large province. The small and scattered population includes many Tibetans and other minority peoples, whose traditional breeds of sheep and other animals are now being improved. Chemical industries are being developed near the great salt lake of Qinghai (the Mongolian name for it is Kokonor, which means "Blue Sea"). The lake is rich in fish and the new fishing industry is an important source of food for the people. Canning and other local industries are also growing.

The people of Xinjiang number only about one-hundredth of China's population, but it covers one-sixth of the surface of the whole country. The people belong to fourteen different minority nationalities; two-thirds of them are Uygurs, who are related to the people of Turkey and speak a kind of Turkish. Though there are fine pasture-lands in the north and west, much of the land is desert.

But even the geography of China is changing. Soldiers of the army units stationed in Xinjiang have reclaimed marshes and other waste-land, and set up large numbers of State farms, used chiefly for growing grain and cotton. On these huge farms most of the work is .now done with the help of machines and modern tools, and using modern methods.

The greatest problem in Xinjiang, as in so many parts of China, is the shortage of water. The central government has spent large sums of money to help the local people. Army men and local civilians have sunk many deep wells and installed electric pumps to tap the underground water. New irrigation canals have been dug, and old ones repaired; the mountain snows are melted and the water carefully channelled to the crops. The people feel they are mastering nature at last.

Tens of thousands of young people from all over China have gone to Xinjiang and other parts of the north-west to work on farms and in the oil and other industries. As they settle down there permanently, new towns and villages grow.

Building a reservoir in the Gobi Desert in Xinjiang, to hold water obtained by melting snow from the mountains

Thousands of minority people go from the north-west to other parts of China for specialised studies, and to learn skills in factories (cotton textiles, machine tools and many others) and come back to use their new skills in the development of their own home districts.

The South-west and Tibet

South-west of Shaanxi province lies the great province of Sichuan ("Four Rivers"), a world in itself, with more than 100 million people. Surrounded on all sides by high mountains, it was easy to defend, and in Chinese history has often been an independent kingdom. A traditional road into the province is now followed by the railway line from Baoji (in Shaanzi) to Chengdu (capital of Sichuan). This runs through beautiful mountainous country, with many tunnels; one section of it was China's first electrified railway.

Chengdu lies in the middle of a fertile rice-growing plain, favoured by a warm, moist climate, and watered by one of the oldest irrigation systems in the world. More than two thousand years ago the Min River was artificially divided, so that its water flows rapidly through a network of canals and thence to the fields. The canals eventually join up again and flow into the Yangzi River.

At one time, the canals were cleaned out every winter, and

the dikes repaired, and in the spring a traditional ceremony was held for the reopening of the system. The local magistrate was carried in his sedan chair by relays of men from the head irrigation works at Guanxian to Chengdu, where he was supposed to arrive before the water, to report its coming. In the years since 1949 these irrigation works have been much improved and enlarged.

Almost everything grows in Sichuan. Rice, wheat, cotton, sugar-cane, tobacco, oranges, tea, oil-seeds and the bamboos which are the food of the giant panda. It is also rich in minerals, including coal, iron, oil and many others. Production of salt from the brine pumped up from deep wells and evaporated by burning natural gas from the same wells has gone on in Sichuan for thousands of years. In the west there are rich forests, the timber being floated down on the rivers.

Yet, with all this wealth of resources, most of the ordinary people of the province have often been desperately poor. Like Chinese peasants everywhere, they had to pay very heavy rent or taxes on the little bits of land they cultivated. For almost forty years before 1949 they suffered the rule of the local warlords, who fought each other for power and made the peasants pay the cost of their wars. Sometimes the land tax had to be paid forty years in advance! Often the peasants who grew the bountiful crops of rice had to give it all up as rent or taxes, and eat sweet potatoes or maize themselves.

Since 1949 the authors have seen for themselves how things have changed in Sichuan since they were there first, more

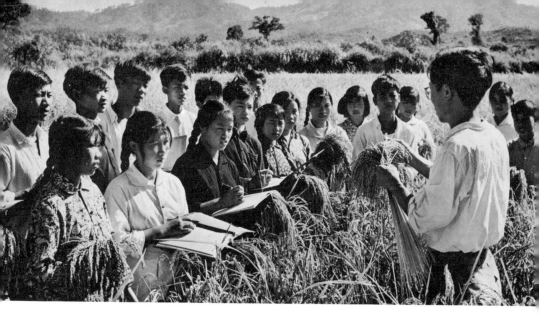

One of the first things a farmer-student must learn about is rice-growing. Here, a practical lesson is in progress

than forty years earlier. Chengdu, Chongqing and other cities are now big industrial centres. But perhaps the biggest change is the dramatic fall in population growth to an average of below one per cent a year, although the national minority peoples are encouraged to *increase* in numbers. The Tibetan population, for example, is growing by two per cent every year, and other minority peoples likewise.

Chongqing, a major trading city built on the solid rock between the Yangzi River and its tributary, the Jialing, was well known (as Chungking) from 1938 to 1946, when it was Chiang Kai-shek's wartime capital.

Dockers and porters in Chongqing used to carry fantastically heavy loads on their shoulder-poles, up and down the

61

hundreds of steep steps from the river, chanting in time with their slow struggling movements.

In the years following 1949 many cableways were built to relieve human beings of this inhuman toil. The city has been transformed in other ways too. New blocks of houses have replaced the dangerous matsheds built on poles which, in the old days, caught fire again and again, making thousands homeless. Many fine roads have been built, buses and trolley-buses (many driven by women) have replaced rickshaws and sedan chairs.

To the east of Chongqing, the Yangzi cuts its way down through the famous gorges up which wooden boats used to be pulled by men straining at ropes. In the past many a ship has been wrecked in the dangerous rapids there. The channel has now been improved by blasting away the rocks and marking it with buoys and signals, so that ships can navigate safely night and day; all the way down to Shanghai, the Yangzi is a broad highway linking the heart of China with the sea.

South of Chongqing the road leads to Guizhou. It used to be said of this province that there were "not three *li* (one mile/1,600 metres) of level ground, never three days without rain, and no inhabitant with three ounces of silver". A poor province indeed. But in natural resources it is by no means poor, and today the face of the province is changing.

Guizhou has more overcast days than any other part of the country; it is not for nothing that its south-western neighbour is called Yunnan ("South of the Clouds"). The eastern part of Yunnan province is a plateau, mild in winter and cool in summer. With its pleasant climate and beautiful lake and mountain scenery, it is likely to become a popular holiday resort. The western half of Yunnan is a wild region through which the Yangzi, Lancang (Mekong) and Nu (Salween) Rivers, here squeezed tightly together between high mountains, cut their way before spreading out to follow widely differing courses to the sea.

Yunnan is like a huge botanical garden; many of its plants are, in fact, to be seen in gardens all over the world. It has more than 10,000 distinct seed-plants, ranging from tropical ones in the south-western valleys to those which grow below the perpetual snow peaks farther north.

There are many national minorities in Yunnan, more than in any other province. The resources of the province include coal and iron and other metals, especially tin. Industries based on these minerals are developing. Many special research institutes, for botany, meteorology, astronomy and linguistics, have been established in Yunnan.

To the north-west of Yunnan lies the high plateau of Tibet, a part of China which many people look at in a rather special way. Because Tibet has been isolated and difficult to get to, we are apt to have romantic notions about it.

In fact, Chinese influence started in Tibet 1,300 years ago, when the princess Wen Cheng of the Tang imperial house married the feudal ruler of Tibet. Later, in about 1250, Kublai Khan made Tibet part of China. More Tibetans live in neighbouring Chinese provinces (Xinjiang, Qinghai and Sichuan) than in Tibet itself.

Tibet is now an autonomous region within China. Great changes have taken place and today the "Roof of the World" is becoming part of the modern world. In the south of the region, where the climate is less severe, many new crops have been introduced. Many industries are being developed, some run by hydro-electric power. Motor-cars and lorries now travel where formerly the only wheel known was the Buddhist lama's prayer wheel. Tibet's capital Lhasa is linked with the rest of China by highway and by air, and tourists can now go there.

Kwangtung and Kwangsi

To round off this bird's-eye view of China let's take a look at China's two southernmost provinces, Guangdong and Guangxi. Guangdong is densely populated, particularly the delta of the Zhujiang (Pearl River), a very fertile area. Because of the difficulty of gaining a livelihood in the old days, many people from this area used to emigrate abroad, especially after they were officially allowed to do so in 1860. They almost always travelled from Guangzhou, the capital of the province, which for centuries was the most important trading port of China. When asked where they came from, they would say the name of the province: "Guangdong", and this word became simplified into "Canton", the name commonly used for Guangzhou.

All over the world there are Chinese people whose parents, grandparents, or great-grandparents came from Guangdong. "Chinese food" outside China is generally food cooked in Cantonese style, and when we hear people speaking Chinese it is probably the Cantonese dialect; this sounds quite different from *putonghua*, which is the common speech of China as a whole.

The tea-houses are a traditional feature of life in Guangzhou; they sell all kinds of delicacies, as well as tea. It is interesting to note that our word *tea* (in its original pronunciation of "tay" still used by the Irish, French and other peoples) represents a Fujian pronunciation of the Chinese word, because tea first came to north-west Europe from Fujian. The standard pronunciation, in northern China and also in Guangzhou, is "cha", and this is used by the Russians (who imported tea in the form of "bricks" overland from north China) and the Portuguese, who met the Cantonese name when they settled at Macao (near the mouth of the Pearl River).

The Canton delta is very fertile, growing two or three crops of rice a year in its semi-tropical climate. Sugar-cane and tropical fruits are also very important crops. There are a great number of fish-ponds in the region, too; mulberry trees, the leaves of which are fed to silkworms, grow on the banks of the ponds. Along the long coastline, the sea fisheries are an important source of food, and the mountains in the north of the province are rich in minerals.

With the heavy tropical rainfall of southern China, a great volume of water has to be drained away by the Pearl River. Although its basin is only two-thirds the area of the Yellow River basin, it discharges eight times as much water into the sea. In the 1950s and 1960s, a large-scale electrically operated drainage and irrigation system was constructed, to irrigate and improve the land, and safeguard the crops.

In the same period, local industry was greatly developed, including mining, iron and steel, and machine-building. Pineapples, lichees and other fruits are canned in several large plants; food products form an important part of China's exports. Hainan Island, which is part of Guangdong, produces a great variety of tropical crops, including rubber, coffee and oil-palms; it also has many minerals.

To the west of Guangdong lies Guangxi autonomous region, with a rather similar climate and range of products; but with

Threshing rice by a traditional method

A platform at the Beijing railway station

a smaller population than Guangdong. Seven million of its people are Zuangs, the most numerous national minority people in the whole country, and Guangxi is now a Zuang autonomous region.

Two links, one old and one new, between China and her neighbour Vietnam pass through Guangxi. The new one is a railway, which runs south-westwards from Hengyang on the Beijing-Guangzhou line, through Guilin (former capital of Guangxi) and Nanning (its present capital) across the border to Hanoi, the capital of Vietnam.

The old link is an extraordinary and beautiful formation of jagged mountains which rise up steeply out of the plain. This limestone formation extends in a great chain, from Guizhou province (north of Guangxi) right down to the coast of Vietnam and into the sea. Nobody who has seen the landscape of Guangxi, especially around Guilin, will find the soaring beauty of the mountains in Chinese landscape paintings at all surprising.

Peasant Farmers and People's Communes

Who owns the land? Who benefits from it? How is it cultivated? Throughout China's history the answers to these questions have decided the fate of dynasties and governments. Since 1949 there have been many changes in the organisation of the countryside—from landlord ownership to peasant ownership, then to co-operatives, then to communes and, since 1980, to management by individual peasant families.

China's vast population includes 800 million peasants; i.e., about four in every five people. They are farmers, but not usually on a large scale. Originally, the great majority of Chinese peasants had no land. Most of the land was owned by landlords, and the peasants had to rent it from them at very high interest; this interest was equal to the value of as much as seventy per cent of the crops. Even if the peasants did own land, they had to pay taxes and a host of other dues to the government. If they were fortunate, a good harvest was just enough to keep the peasant and his family alive. But such good luck came rarely.

Ploughing with a water buffalo, near Chengdu. In the background is the gateway of a former ancestral temple. Tractors are also used: the small "walking" models are very popular for haulage as well as cultivation

The long history of China records that there were floods or drought somewhere in every year. The peasant had no means to pay rent or taxes and had to borrow money, at very high interest (sometimes as much as one hundred per cent a *month*) in order to buy seeds for the next sowing.

In this way, the average farmer got poorer and poorer. He had no hope of improving his crops, because he had no money to buy an ox or more tools, let alone fertiliser. In famine years many families were wiped out by starvation and disease. Very often a whole village became deserted as the

69

A dairy farm near Beijing

few survivors left their poor homes and roamed about as beggars.

Often the farmer had to pay his debts by selling his children to the landlord; sometimes he suffered beatings or even death at the hands of the landlord's bailiffs. The misery and cruelty were intolerable. That is why so many peasants drowned their baby girls. Boy babies had a better chance, because it was hoped they would survive to work and carry on the family.

In this century, people who made a study of China came to realise that her greatest problem was the condition of the peasants. Without land of their own they could not grow enough food for their own families—let alone for the whole country. Dr. Sun Yat-sen, "Father" of the Chinese (1911) Revolution, formulated the policy of "land to the tiller" but he was not able to put it into practice.

The scholar who was able to apply his knowledge in practice was Mao Zedong, himself the son of a peasant. He made a thorough study of the peasant question in his native province of Hunan and wrote a report which became a historic document.

During the war against the Japanese invaders, the Chinese Red Army (or People's Liberation Army) was made up of peasants. As they fought their guerrilla war from village to village against the Japanese and against Chiang Kai-shek's government troops, they helped organise the villagers into peasant associations to divide the land, and set up local governments behind the enemy lines.

Mao Zedong and many of his colleagues had already gained experience in organising "land reform"; i.e., dividing the land. In 1950 the new Central People's Government proclaimed the Land Law. Tens of thousands of teachers and students were sent out into the villages to work closely with the peasants who could not read or write. They measured the land and classified it into different grades and calculated the

Rural housing near Shenyang

total population of the areas, including babies. It was a very complicated process, as they wanted to be fair to everyone.

After many discussions it was decided, during 1955–6, to form agricultural co-operatives all over the country. All the land was pooled together and when the crops were harvested owners were paid dividends on their shares. Draught animals were dealt with in the same way. A member's own hours of work on the farm were counted and paid for accordingly.

In this new organisation there was more money to buy tools and seeds and more labour to work according to a common plan. The result was bigger crops, which increased the peasants' trust and enthusiasm for the co-operatives. They were able to make more ambitious plans for irrigation works, land drainage, tree-planting or keeping animals, according to the locality.

They worked hard and achieved a lot in the first two or three years. But there were snags in their large-scale planning. A stream might run across the land of several co-operatives. A mountain might have too much water on one side and none on the other. The farms were still divided into small areas, and would never be suitable for machines. The co-operatives still had too few people and too little money to work on a really large scale.

So, in 1978, very soon after the formation of co-operatives, leaders in several parts of the country, encouraged by Chairman Mao Zedong, linked them together to form very much bigger organizations. These were called people's communes,

72

A modern piggery

and they replaced the *xiang* (township) at the lowest level of government (below the county). Under the 1982 Constitution, townships have again replaced communes.

Each commune brought together several "production brigades". These still exist; under them come the production teams. A team is made up of the families living in a hamlet. The brigade is the size of the former village. The whole township may number 10,000 to 20,000 people, or more, and there are many townships in each county.

The team is organised according to the nature of the work. For example, in different parts of the country its main crop may be rice or wheat, cotton or sugar-cane, or tea; subsidiary lines may be pigs, fish-ponds, or rearing silkworms. The team divides the members into groups for different jobs according to their age and physical condition.

In the years after 1958 the communes and production brigades were responsible for almost everything in the countryside, including food production, running local industry and afforesting the bare mountains. They were responsible for educating the children (and adults, who never had education before) and for medical services; and they organised the militia. When disasters such as drought or flood happened, they (with the help of the army) could organise large numbers of people to deal with the emergency.

But many communes (often because of undemocratic leadership) failed to mobilise the initiative of the peasants; food production grew more slowly than population. Since 1980 a "responsibility system" has been introduced. Under this, the land still belongs to the team but its cultivation is divided among households, each responsible for growing a fixed amount of produce for the state. After contributions to the common welfare funds, any surplus over this amount is kept by the family. Thus, if they produce more grain, cotton, vegetables, pigs, fish or anything else, they get more money. Standards of living in the countryside have risen greatly, and some peasants have become rich.

74

Inside the Wuhan steelworks

Industrial China

In 1907 an American missionary to China wrote the following prophetic words:

"Under new conditions impelled by fresh impulses we behold the wonderful spectacle of the most ancient and the most populous of empires with one hand clinging to the mighty past, while with the other groping for a perhaps still more mighty future. . . .

"The Chinese may be said to be equipped for that future as no other people now is or perhaps ever has been. The development of their immense natural resources has not as yet seriously begun. Scientific agriculture for soils and for seeds, the improvement of old plants and the introduction of new ones, the plantation of forests on now barren mountains, the deepening and broadening of the countless artificial waterways, modern engineering methods employed to remove rapids and other obstructions to navigation, the construction of reservoirs to control the flood waters of the great rivers, the general introduction of railways and of steam power—these and other innovations will make a new physical China, put an end to famines, and enable the country to support several times its present population with far less difficulty than is now felt.

"For the new industries which will thus be developed the Chinese are almost ideally fitted. The Chinese eye, hand and brain, by ages of experience in almost every direction, are already trained, and can easily be rendered still more expert so as to do anything which anybody can do anywhere."

Every one of these words of Arthur Smith has proved true, but it took much longer than he expected.

We know that the Chinese invented the water-clock, astronomical instruments, printing, the compass and very many other things, hundreds of years before they were known in

This huge hydraulic press made by a shipyard in Shanghai can forge 300 tonne steel ingots

Europe. The Chinese also made many important discoveries, including such fundamental things as the best way of harnessing a horse, deep-drilling and how to cast iron. Yet, in the writers' youth, the peasants in the villages had given up their cotton-weaving, because people were buying cheap cloth, first from Lancashire and later from British or Japanese factories in Shanghai or Hankou.

Since 1949 things have been quite different. Now China makes huge machines, complicated tools, precision instruments for scientific and medical uses, and countless other highly reliable products. There are Trade Fairs in Guangzhou and elsewhere; thousands of foreign businessmen come, to sign contracts for exports or imports. Those who come regularly notice the improvement in the variety and quality of the goods from year to year. People often ask: "Where and how does China train the workers and find the engineers?" and "Where does the money come from?"

In the first place, the Chinese factories provide scientific, technological and general education for all their workers. This applies to all, from those who never learned to read and write before, right through to those who have been in school for many years, and are already working as engineers. Tens of thousands have gone through such courses.

There is another very important practice. If a factory has made a new and outstanding achievement, other similar factories all over the country send representatives there to see it, so that they can learn to do the same. The factory also sends

A worker in a small rural factory

A worker in a textile mill

out its own workers and engineers, who achieved the success, to help other factories.

In new China, almost all the industry belongs to the government or to co-operative groups; no private person takes any of the profits made by factories. These are all used for public purposes: to build more factories, extract more minerals from the earth, and make more tractors, farm tools and fertilisers for the farms, as well as consumer goods of all kinds. The cost of national defence must also be met, and there is an insatiable demand for textiles, plastics, electronics—and indeed all kinds of consumer goods.

China relies mainly on her own efforts to industrialise the country. In the years after 1949 she received much technical assistance and equipment from the Soviet Union (all of which she paid for) but this ended in 1960.

The Chinese government is encouraging many new ways of developing the country's economy and raising the people's standard of living. The "responsibility system" successfully adopted in the countryside is being extended to industry and trade as well. In the towns young people without regular jobs are trained and helped to start small co-operative businesses e.g. tailoring, bicycle repair, restaurants. Thus the public get better service and the individuals earn their living.

City Life and Entertainment

The life of the Chinese people, like that of peoples everywhere in the world, is centred on the home and the family. But, of course, there are many differences too between life in modern China and life in other countries.

To begin with, the arrangement of the houses is different.

Traditional Chinese houses are built in a series of rooms round the three or four sides of a courtyard. In old China a rich family was really a whole clan. Three or four, or even five generations lived together—all the sons and grandsons and their wives—and the oldest generation (grandparents or great-grandparents) ruled over the whole clan.

From the day of their birth children were the precious *common* possession of the whole huge household. The child grew up as a member of a large community. Even if the family was a small one, different households lived around a communal courtyard and shared each other's lives. Children played together and had a sense of belonging to one another.

But there were serious drawbacks in this old family system. The worst of them was that all the younger generation had to obey the head of the clan-family. It was impossible for young men to develop their own talents and initiative; they were not even allowed to choose their own wives. Women and girls

A typical courtyard in a traditional Beijing house

were far worse off. Not many had a chance to learn to read and write, even in very rich families. They had to obey their mothers-in-law, as well as their husbands and their own parents.

There was another serious drawback, too. Since it was difficult to get a job, the bread-winner of the family had to feed too many people, often including distant cousins. These jobless people lived as parasites. Family relationships became unfriendly and selfish and nerves became strained, leading to frequent quarrels and brawls. Students who had received a modern education bitterly resented being forced by their parents and grandparents into marrying uneducated girls. They rebelled, and in that way the old clan-family started to break up. This break-up began during the early years of the twentieth century.

Even more drastic changes have occurred in the years since 1949. In the first place, young men and women now have their own jobs which may take them far away from their home-town. Secondly, in modern China no man or woman can be forced to marry against his or her own wishes. Each marries the person of his or her own choice, and the new couple live wherever their work is. Thus the old clan system has finally broken up, but even today the Chinese believe that little children grow up more healthily if they have their grandparents living with them and that the old folk are happier in their old age to have their grandchildren around.

So in modern China the family is small. It often consists

A popular street game: the Chinese version of skipping, using elastic cords instead of rope

of three generations—the parents, their children and one or two grandparents, usually on the father's side. If the young couple go to a distant place to work, the old parents may prefer to stay behind and live with another son or daughter.

In the cities many blocks of flats are built, usually near factories. The Chinese workers and their families are proud of them, because for the first time they have proper homes with modern amenities, instead of the old mud huts or makeshift hovels. There are always nurseries and schools near by, as well as parks and playgrounds, a cinema, a bank, a post office, a cultural centre and, of course, shops. If a young mother decides to take a job she can leave her toddler in the nursery school for a few hours or even longer. In order to slow down the rise in population, China now has a "single child family" policy, but the number of children born will go on increasing for years to come.

Whether people live in the traditional houses or in blocks of flats there is always a neighbourhood committee, formed by representatives from the houses around a courtyard, or from each lane, street or block. Most members of such committees are retired people; some are married women who do not work full time.

The committee looks after such things as public health, cleaning the streets and other public places (including stairways in blocks of flats), general social welfare and the welfare of old people who have no children or grandchildren to take care of them.

If there is no public park or children's centre near by, the

This boy is actually playing Chinese chess, not draughts

neighbourhood committee often arranges activities in one of the homes, after school hours, so that the children can enjoy their hobbies or do their homework together.

On Sundays, if the weather is fine, city families all over China stroll in the parks, bathe or skate, according to the season, go to the theatre or cinema, do their family shopping or enjoy a good dinner in a restaurant. Sometimes young people will spend the day at the "cultural palace", learning to paint, practising music and dancing, playing chess, or reading in the library. And young children do the same, with the help of specialist tutors, in their own centres. Grandparents often go with their grandchildren to the parks or museums. Another popular activity on Sundays is visiting relatives or friends, or eating out, or simply sitting in tea-houses.

The Chinese theatre—which includes plays, operas, dancing, singing, puppet plays and acrobatics—has a long tradition and has always been popular throughout history. There was a time, however, when the rather strict "puritan" taste of some Confucian scholars led them to condemn the popular theatre and to influence their followers not to patronise it.

This meant that, as time went on, the artists were driven to perform only for the poor and uneducated people who ignored the views of the scholarly officials and who loved the traditional entertainment. The actual theatres were usually quite small, holding only a few hundred people. But often performances were also given in the market-places, the tea-houses and the Buddhist temples during festivals.

85

Fireworks were invented in China and they are still a popular part of all public celebrations. This photograph was taken in Beijing on the national holiday on 1st October

Touring entertainers travelled from village to village and performed in the open air. The village folk would bring their own benches to sit on, or would just stand and watch. While tickets were sold in advance and there were fixed charges for entrance in the town theatres, the village audiences merely contributed what they thought they could afford when the hat was passed round. Chinese people love the theatre and cinema. Factories, colleges and government departments often get big blocks of tickets for their workers or students. New plays and films on past history and present problems of life and work are being produced very widely. There are amateur groups everywhere, in schools, communes and factories, but the government has also built many fine permanent concert halls and theatres. Today, artists are no longer dependent on the whims of their village audiences; they are now paid a regular wage and can train in special schools to become proficient in both traditional and modern theatrical skills.

The sound of music or stories from a transistor radio entertaining its owner working in the fields is quite common. Television cannot yet be received everywhere but is spreading rapidly; in cities, viewers have a choice of programme. Both radio and television have scientific and other educational programmes which are followed by millions of people; they play a very important part in the modernisation of China.

Education

In the Oriental departments of many university libraries throughout the world there are hundreds of thousands of volumes of Chinese classics, both in the original Chinese texts and translated into various foreign languages. Much has also been written in foreign languages *about* the life and work of Chinese scholars, and research is being done all the time both in China and abroad.

The reason for this great interest is that the works of learned Chinese classical scholars provide almost inexhaustible research material on philosophy, history, literature and many other subjects. There is, for instance, the teaching of Confucius (551–479 B.C.) about human relationships, and the theory of Mencius (fourth century. B.C.) that human nature was fundamentally good. Another scholar, Wang Anshi (A.D. 1021–1086), produced a whole theory and programme for just and reasonable government.

A complete list of such scholars and their work would be endless. The system of competitive examinations for the Chinese civil service goes back to the third century B.C. These examinations were designed to test the scholar's knowledge of the Confucian classics. At its best, the system produced many able, honest and fearless scholar-officials, some of whom are famous in Chinese history. The system had such a high reputation that in the nineteenth century it inspired Western nations to introduce competitive examinations for *their* civil services.

Yet, after more than two thousand years of this educational system, the great majority (about eighty-five per cent) of the population could not read or write, because they were too poor to pay for any education. The small minority of learned people were generally the sons of landowners. After studying the classics and passing examinations, they became officials, and enjoyed political power and accumulated wealth for their clan-families.

A strong Emperor could maintain his power through them, but the peasants often rebelled against the officials, especially in bad times. In the nineteenth century, when China was

Children's clubs like this are to be found all over China

being defeated again and again by foreign powers, it became clear that the system could not last any longer. Han officials at the Manchu Court demanded that the ancient educational system should be changed. Finally, in 1906, orders were issued that it should be replaced by a modern, Western system.

A number of Western-style schools were started and, by 1949, there were a number of schools and colleges modelled on those of the United States, Britain, France, etc. Christian missionaries and their supporters, especially in America, felt that the Chinese demand for modern education should be met by mission schools and colleges.

But though the mission schools did give some education to the middle classes, it was often not at all suited to China. The nation-wide change in education only began after 1949.

After the establishment of the People's Government in 1949, ideas about education completely changed. It was maintained that every person should have the chance for education in order to develop his or her character and talent. Education was considered essential for building the new socialist society.

Obviously, the new government could not immediately build schools for the whole population (of which eighty-five per cent were previously illiterate). It did not have the money, the buildings, the teaching materials or the teachers. It tried its best to build schools and train teachers, and made the most of all available resources and materials for makeshift day and evening classes. It enlisted anyone with some schooling to teach those with none. In this way, everyone was encouraged to learn and to teach at the same time.

Children in the nursery school attached to a textile mill

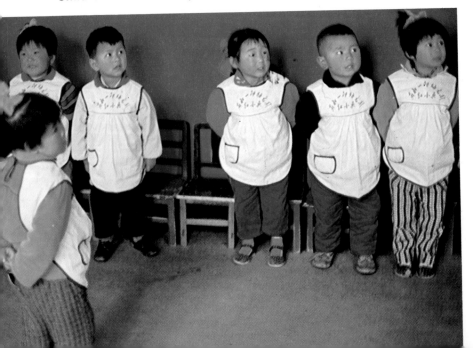

Students receiving technical training

Now, more than seventy-five per cent of the population can read and write. Many of them have become agricultural scientists or industrial engineers. The picture is completely different from that before 1949. In 1978 there was a National Science Conference. Thousands of people attended it; there were commune members, industrial workers and members of the armed forces, as well as teachers and scientific research workers. The Conference made plans to develop the study of science and technology as much as possible; this is being done through radio, the television university, spare-time classes and correspondence courses.

Soon afterwards a National Educational Work Conference was held for the purpose of raising the standard of education.

As in every field of Chinese life, there have been many changes in education since 1949. The idea that we should all work with our hands as well as our brains is a good one which has to be emphasized strongly in China (traditional education was a way of escaping from hard manual work). But in the "Cultural Revolution" (1966-76) it was taken much too far. A whole generation of young people lost their chance of education while they worked in the countryside, sometimes for many years.

This was very serious not only for them personally but for the country, which needs more and more highly trained people to lead it in modernisation. A big programme of expansion and improvement of schools and colleges is under way, but only a small proportion of school-leavers can go on to work for degrees in colleges and universities. Long- and short-term courses of all kinds are being organised at different levels, not only for city people but also for peasants in the countryside.

Early in 1983 there was much discussion in the newspapers and at special conferences about how to make secondary schools and colleges serve the needs of rural construction and modern development better, and also on how to improve primary education which is still very backward in many country areas.

Raising the all-round educational level of the whole population is perhaps China's most vital long-term task.

China in the World Today

Since 1971, China's importance in the world has continued to grow. Although a poor country itself, China gives aid to more than sixty other countries, usually in the form of small-scale agricultural projects which the local people can manage themselves. But Chinese workers have also built textile mills and electric power stations. They have also constructed new roads and countless bridges. The largest and most famous aid project is the Tanzam Railway linking Tanzania and Zambia. Appropriately, it is called the Friendship Railway.

Thousands of people from all over the world visit China every year: some to study various subjects from fish farming to herbal medicine and acupuncture; others to see the great changes which have taken place. China has certainly come a very long way since the time when the country was described by foreigners as the "sick man of Asia".

Some of the strongest criticisms of China come from people who think that there is no "individual freedom" there and that there is too much "regimentation". The Chinese reply is that in working together to build their country anew they are creating far better human relationships, and that the individual can only develop fully by working and living in the

93

Cleaning and examining some of the life-size figures which are recently discovered relics of the Qin dynasty—"new" China takes a pride in "old" China

community. This emphasis fits in very well with the traditional Confucian ideal of a world in harmony. Thus the new China takes inspiration from, but also revolutionises, the old, as it enters the modern world.

Index